FUNDAMENTAL RIGHTS

FUNDAMENTAL RIGHTS

DR TAMANA BAHLOL

Copyright © Dr Tamana Bahlol
All Rights Reserved.

This book has been published with all efforts taken to make the material error-free after the consent of the author. However, the author and the publisher do not assume and hereby disclaim any liability to any party for any loss, damage, or disruption caused by errors or omissions, whether such errors or omissions result from negligence, accident, or any other cause.

While every effort has been made to avoid any mistake or omission, this publication is being sold on the condition and understanding that neither the author nor the publishers or printers would be liable in any manner to any person by reason of any mistake or omission in this publication or for any action taken or omitted to be taken or advice rendered or accepted on the basis of this work. For any defect in printing or binding the publishers will be liable only to replace the defective copy by another copy of this work then available.

Contents

Acknowledgements

- **Fundamental rights** are a group of rights that have been recognized by a high degree of protection from encroachment. These rights are specifically identified in a constitution,

  Fundamental rights are the rights that are essential for the overall development of the people of the nation. These rights are granted to each and every citizen of the nation from birth, without any discrimination on basis of caste, creed, sex, and religion.

-     Fundamental rights play a very significant role in the life of any citizen. These rights can defend during the time of complexity & difficulty and help us grow into a good human being and that's why all the rights are the needs of people. This right is a very special right given to all the citizens. According to this right, a citizen has the power to go to the court in case of denial of any of the fundamental rights. The court stands as a guard for anybody against the breach of these rights.

- Fundamental rights are a group of rights that have been recognized by a high degree of protection from encroachment. These rights are specifically identified in a constitution, Fundamental rights are the rights that are essential for the overall development of the people of the nation. These rights are granted to each and every citizen of the nation from birth, without any discrimination on basis of caste, creed, sex, and religion. Fundamental rights are a group of rights that have been recognized by the Supreme Court as requiring a high degree of protection from government encroachment. These rights are specifically identified in the Constitution (especially in the Bill of Rights), or have been found under Due Process. Fundamental Rights are the basic human rights given to a country's citizens. These rights are justiciable; if someone doesn't abide by these rights, they can be subjected to a court of law. These rights are stated in Part III of the Constitution. Fundamental rights help in the development of the State. The Fundamental Rights are a list of rights that help in the development of the citizens in a country. Fundamental rights are enforceable by the court of law. Fundamental rights help in making a State, a Welfare State. A Welfare State promotes and facilitates the wellbeing of its citizens. There are six fundamental rights in total, Rights to equality, right to freedom, and right to constitutional remedies. However, only providing fundamental rights is not enough; they have to be safeguarded. The fundamental rights apply to all the people living in the country, irrespective of caste, creed, gender, social status, and so on. Fundamental rights that are incorporated in our constitution forms the basis of our existence in the country. Without them being present, things like dissent and objection could have been difficult. The fact that they are justifiable and thus enforceable by courts make them an instrument of power in the hands of the common man. The Government can suspend the clauses under which they operate fundamental rights in times of an emergency, which can be harmful and dangerous. Can you imagine a life where there is no freedom to speak, live, or do the things of our choice? But it is not so, we have been granted some fundamental rights by our constitution. These rights are important for the development of an individual. Nobody can be exploited or discriminated against on any basis. These rights do not provide freedom to do anything that disrupts the unity of the nation. These rights form an important part of the constitution which breaching is a punishable act. Fundamental rights are the rights that are essential for the overall development of the people of the nation. These rights are granted to each and every citizen of the nation from birth, without any discrimination on basis of caste, creed, sex, and religion. The violation of fundamental rights is a punishable offense. The person can directly go to the court for the justice of breaching of the fundamental right. The fundamental right grants us the freedom to live happily and do whatever we desire. The only thing that people need to remember is that their freedom should not become a nuisance in other's freedom. Historical Fundamental Rights In 1789, "The Declaration of Rights of Man" was adopted by the French National Assembly. The United States Constitution included a section on Fundamental Rights. The United Nations General Assembly adopted the Universal Declaration of Human Rights, which was made in December 1948. It included social, economic, political and cultural rights of the people. The suggestion of incorporating religious and cultural rights in the form of basic rights of citizens in India was given in 1928 by the report of the Nehru Committee. However, the Simon Commission did not support this idea of incorporating fundamental rights into the Constitution. In the session organized in Karachi in 1931, the Indian National Congress again asked for a written assurance in fundamental rights (fundamental 8 rights) in constitutional arrangements that would be made in future in world . The demand for fundamental rights was emphasized at the Round Table Conference held in London. Later in the second round table conference, Mahatma Gandhi had demanded protection for the protection of Indian culture, language, script, profession, education and religious practices and the rights of minorities. After independence in 1947, the Constituent Assembly took an oath for future good governance. It demanded a Constitution which guarantees the action of all people of India - Justice, Social, Economic and Political Equality, Equal Opportunities, Freedom of View, Expression, Trust, Union, Business and Law and Public Ethics. . At the same time, a guarantee of special facilities was also given to minorities, backward classes and scheduled castes. Fundamental rights are not absolute, they are subject to reasonable limits. They target stability between an individual's independence and social security, but proper restrictions are subject to legal review. Here's a look at some specific features of these rights: o All fundamental rights can be suspended. During the Emergency, the right to freedom is automatically suspended in the interest of the country's security and integrity. o Many fundamental rights are for Indian citizens, but the benefit of some fundamental rights can be raised by both citizens and noncitizens of the country. o Fundamental rights can be amended but they cannot be terminated. The elimination of fundamental rights will violate the fundamental principle of the Constitution. o Fundamental Rights are both positive and negative. Negative powers prevent the country from doing certain things. This prevents the country from discriminating. o Some rights are available against the country. Some rights are available against the people. o Fundamental rights are justifiable. If a citizen's fundamental rights are violated, he can go to court. o Some basic rights are not available to those working in defense services because they are restricted from some rights. Fundamental Rights are political and social in nature. The citizens of India have not been guaranteed any economic rights, although their rights without them are trivial or inconclusive. Each rights are related to some duties. Fundamental rights have a broad perspective and they protect our social, economic, cultural and religious interests. These are an integral part of the Constitution. It cannot be altered or removed from common law. Fundamental rights are an essential part of our constitution. Twenty-four articles are included with these basic rights. Parliament can amend fundamental rights through a special process. The purpose of fundamental right is to restore collective interest with personal interest. The right provides equality to everyone in the nation. The right helps in the growth and development of the people in the nation. The development of people will also ensure the progress Fundamental rights are essential for the people to live in peace and harmony in the nation. These rights also confer some duties on the citizens of the nation that must be done appropriately. Society as well as the nation. Right to self-determination Right to liberty Right to due process of law Right to freedom of movement Right to privacy Right to freedom of thought Right to freedom of religion Right to freedom of expression Right to peaceful assembly Right to freedom of association The right to equality The right to freedom The right against exploitation The right to freedom of religion The Cultural and educational The right to constitutional remedies The right to interstate travel The right to parent one's children The right to privacy The right to marriage The right of self-defense The Fundamental Rights Agency The Inalienable rights The Universal human rights Freedom of speech Freedom of expression Freedom of assembly without arms Freedom of association Freedom to practice any profession Freedom to reside in any part of the country Right to Equality This right includes the equality before the Law which implies a prohibition of discrimination on the basis of caste, creed, color or sex, equal protection of the law, equal opportunity in public employment and abolition of untouchability and titles. It also states that every citizen shall have equal access to all public places. To provide equal opportunities there will be no reservation in government services except in the case of scheduled caste, scheduled tribes, and other backward classes and for war widows and physically handicapped person. This right was made to abolish untouchability which was practiced in India for decades. Right to Freedom This right includes the right to freedom of speech, freedom of expression, and freedom to form unions and associations. It also includes freedom to travel anywhere in world freedom to live in any part of world and the freedom to choose any profession of their interest. This right also states that any citizen of India has the full right to purchase, sell and hold property in any part of the country. According to these rights, people will have the liberty to indulge in any trade or business. This right also defines that a person cannot be convicted twice for the same offense and it also cannot be compelled to stand as a witness against oneself. Right against Exploitation This right includes the prohibition of any form of forced labor. Children who are below the age of 14 years are not allowed to work in mines or factories where the risk of life is involved. According to these rights, no person has the right to exploit the other person in any way. Therefore human trafficking & begging have been made legal offenses and those found involved are to be penalized. According to this rights slavery and traffic among women and children for dishonest purposes has been declared an offense. Payment of minimum wage against the labor is defined and no compromise is allowed in this regard. Right to Freedom of Religion These right states that there will be full freedom of conscience for all citizens of India. All people shall have equal right to freely adopt, practice and spread the religion of their choice. The state shall not hinder in any religious affairs of any individual in any manner. In this, all religions have a right to establish and uphold institutions for religious and charitable purposes. Also, they will be free to manage their own affairs with respect to these rights. Cultural and Educational Right This right is one of the most important rights as education is the primary right of each child. According to this right, all are free to follow the culture of their choice. Also, all are free to get the education of their choice. No individual will be denied admission in any of the educational institutes on the basis of their culture, caste or religion. According to this, all the minorities have the right to establish their own educational institutes. Right to Constitutional Remedy This right is a very special right given to all the citizens. According to this right, a citizen has the power to go to the court in case of denial of any of the fundamental rights. The court stands as a guard for anybody against the breach of these rights. If the government forcefully or intentionally does injustice to any individual or if a person is imprisoned without any reason or by the unlawful act then this right allows the person to go to the court for getting justice against the actions of the government. Legal Obligations No one can be a responsible citizen without staying within the law. It is as simple as that. Criminals, by their very nature, are not behaving as responsible citizens. Laws exist to protect citizens, the communities they live in and their property. So to be a responsible citizen, we must respect these laws and abide by them. Harming others or others' property does not equate to being a good citizen. Social Obligations Social obligations really form the bulk of being a responsible citizen and what this means. To be a responsible citizen, we should help our communities and those who live in them. So, being a responsible citizen can encompass things such as volunteering. Volunteering, the third sector is worth billions to our economy and even more to those who are helped by volunteering. But in the interests of being a responsible citizen, this could include smaller things too. So, volunteering for the Samaritans is a noble job to do and one which is certainly needed. But the elderly lady who lives alone may need someone to do her shopping and this demonstrates responsible citizenship just as much as volunteering in an organization. Other social obligations of being a good citizen can include things such as helping local businesses. This may means buying the meat for Sunday dinner from a local butcher rather than a supermarket, or using a small local bookstore rather than the internet. Being a responsible citizen also means being involved in our communities. This may be demonstrated by being on the school parent teacher association or the village hall committee. It may be as simple as attending events organized by these people. Moral Obligations Moral obligations of being a responsible citizen are harder to pin down because different people have different moral codes. But one place we can all start is in helping the environment. The environmental problems society is facing are of our own making and we all have a moral obligation to do what we can to change this. So by living as environmentally friendly life as possible, we can help fulfill our moral obligations of being a responsible citizen. Taking recyclables to be recycled and using a compost bin are two easy ways and there are many more. And they can be linked in with other obligations. For example, if you have a compose bin but no plants to use the compost on, you could give it to people who have plants but live alone, making them less likely to generate a huge amount of compost themselves. Being a responsible citizen should not be a hard thing but it should be something which occasionally requires a little extra effort. This is because being a responsible citizen is, at its core, about being a less selfish person, and putting the needs of society before your own needs. It does not means you have to sacrifice all your free time to volunteer or help others, but it does means taking a little time to think about the impact of your actions on others. All fundamental rights can be suspended. The right to freedom is automatically suspended during an emergency in the interests of the security and integrity of the country. Fundamental rights can be amended but not abolished. Fundamental rights are both positive and negative. Negative rights prevent the country from doing certain things. It prevents the country from discriminating. Some rights are available against the country. Some rights are available against individuals. Fundamental rights are political and social in nature. Each authority deals with certain duties. Fundamental rights have a broad view and protect our social, economic, cultural and religious interests. They are an integral part of the constitution. Fundamental rights are an essential part of our Constitution. Twenty-four articles are included with these basic rights. Parliament can amend Fundamental Rights through a special process. The fundamental right is intended to restore collective interest along with individual interest.